LETTER
TO A
Grieving
Heart

BILLY SPRAGUE

PHOTOGRAPHY BY JOHN MACMURRAY

HARVEST HOUSE PUBLISHERS
Eugene, Oregon

Letter to a Grieving Heart

Text copyright © 2001 by Billy Sprague

Published by Harvest House Publishers
Eugene, Oregon 97402

Library of Congress Cataloging-in-Publication Data

Sprague, Billy.
    Letter to a grieving heart / Billy Sprague; photography by John MacMurray.
        p. cm.
    ISBN 0-7369-0732-7
        1. Consolation. 2. Bereavement—Religious aspects—Christianity. 3. Grief—Religious
aspects—Christianity. 4. Death—Religious aspects—Christianity. I. Title.
    BV4905.3 .S68 2001
    248.8'66—dc21   2001016983

Design and production by Terry Dugan Design, Minneapolis, Minnesota

Permissions and Acknowledgments

Page 13: "A Ship Out of Water" by Bruce Carroll and Billy Sprague. ©1996 Sony/ATV Tunes; Skin Horse, Inc. (ASCAP).
Used by permission. Page 33: "I Wish" by Billy Sprague. © 1989 Billy Sprague/Skin Horse, Inc. & Edward Grant, Inc. ASCAP.
All rights reserved. Used by permission. Page 34: "Beside You in the Rain" by Jim Weber and Billy Sprague. ©1997 Desperate
Heart Music/Skin Horse, Inc. ASCAP. Used by permission. Page 62: "Til I See You Again" by Billy Sprague & Joe Beck.
© 2000 by Skin Horse, Inc. (ASCAP)/Acuff-Rose Music (BMI). Used by permission. Page 38, 23: "Press On" by Billy Sprague
& Jim Weber. ©1993 Paragon Music Corp.-Skin Horse, Inc./Centergetic Music (admin. by Integrated Copyright Group)
ASCAP. Used by permission.

Verses are taken from the Holy Bible: New International Version.® NIV ®. Copyright ©1973, 1978, 1984 by the International
Bible Society. Used by permission of Zondervan Publishing House.

Manufactured in China

04 05 06 07 08 09 10 /IM/ 10 9 8 7 6 5

This book is dedicated

to the memory of my grandmother,

Myrtle Payne

b. July 31, 1895

d. March 31, 1997

No one can talk away the pain. Grief drains most words of their power anyway.

1

Beyond Words

I am so sorry you have to face life with this kind of wound. I don't have any answers. Or magic words.

In fact, I would rather sit or walk with you for a silent hour than fill your ears with words that ring hollow and fall so short of real comfort. I would rather do your dishes. Or restock your refrigerator. Or write out the checks to pay your bills, answer your phone, or take care of other mundane details. I would rather listen to you tell me all the things you love about the person you are missing so much. Or light a fire in your fireplace and make you something warm to drink. Or read the Psalms to you. Or bring you a pot of homemade soup. I would rather sleep on the floor by your bed so when you wake up in agony, someone is there. Because these are the things that people did for me when grief broke down my door some years ago.

I cannot explain much about anything. I can only compare notes with you about the road we are on. And begin to tell you a few of the hundreds of little things that eased me forward. At times I didn't want to go forward at all. I even wanted to die and go on to heaven, mostly to stop the pain, which I thought would never ease. (I still do long for heaven in many ways, but no longer out of desperation.) That crossing-over will, of course, come in time. As King David said when his infant son died, "I will go to him, but he will not return to me."

No one can talk away the pain. Grief drains most words of their power anyway. But a few words carried great strength for me. Jesus spoke about and promised to prepare a great reunion. His words always held a great power and gave me hope for an eternal gathering with those I love. Those words have become even more powerful each time someone I love leaves this life—a

favorite college professor whose heart stopped while sitting at his typewriter...my fiancée in a car wreck...my wife's aunt, in a battle with cancer at the age of forty-two...my Grandmother Myrtle, who slipped away peacefully in her sleep a few months before her one hundred and second birthday. Naturally, the thought of seeing all of them again after this life became an even stronger hope.

But what about until heaven? How do you drag a heavy, frozen heart around every day and night? It's exhausting. Like a fever. But cold. And you think you will never feel very much again. Except the pain.

For two years after my fiancée's death, the thawing of my heart was agonizingly slow. This sort of awakening is, for most, subtle in

I was down in the valley
   of the shadow of death
Where the passion for life
   drained like blood from my chest
And it took more than my will just
   to take a step
When the compass of hope
   was gone

In a darkness so black that I wished
   for the blues
Every desperate prayer
   seemed like heaven refused
And some days I found faith meant
   just tying my shoes
And it was all I could do
   to press on

coming, and for good reason. (In fact, I suspect those who seem to bounce back too quickly are trying to put a better face on the pain in their hearts.) "Little by little we come alive," Frederick Buechner wrote. This especially applies to grief. The heavy, invisible cloak is a fog that gives way so stubbornly, we are convinced it will never lift.

In my experience, the landscape ahead was shrouded in uncertainty. I couldn't see one day ahead of me. I became a foot watcher, walking through airports or the grocery store staring at my feet, methodically moving through a misty world. One foot, then the other. Even before that I came to associate faith with simply tying my shoes. Some days, especially early on, it was the only act of faith I could muster.

Maybe you are stronger than I was. Maybe you are already tying your shoes and running again. Or maybe you can't even concentrate long enough to finish this page and are not ready for much of what I have to say here.

For now, you may find more comfort in the photographs. (But I found even the natural beauty of this world can bring both comfort and an exquisite pain amid the intensity of grief. Maybe that's because beauty and love overlap so much.) Even so, I find myself pouring all this out for what it's worth. Don't rush it. The Spirit of God must know what we can handle and is, whether we sense it or not, accompanying (sometimes carrying) each of us along this lovely, dangerous journey. And in some sense, I don't doubt that those who are with him are pulling for us, too.

Over a year after RosaLynn's death, I took a walk in the woods with a friend. There is something about the muted light filtered through the leaves of a forest canopy and the muffled sound of footsteps on the cushioned ground that softens the world. A forest seems reverent, as if it knows your sorrow.

As we walked, this happily married father of two told me, "I want to tell you something you might not want to hear right now and may not believe."

"What's that?" I said, ready to discard almost any "advice."

"The heart is larger than you think."

What he meant was that a lot of people can live in one heart. All those we love occupy a unique place inside us. Forever. His obvious implication for my situation was that some-day I could love again. Love can make more room.

My friend was right. I didn't want to hear it. Not at the time. But he had the credibility of someone who knew personal grief. He had lost the woman he intended to marry fifteen years earlier to leukemia.

Certainly, the challenge for some is to love again, especially those who lose a spouse or a lover, but for all of us who must send some-one we love on ahead, the struggle is more about coming fully alive again. So, I heard the words my friend kindly offered and tucked them away for another time.

You may need to do that with this book. For now, simply take in the photographs, like scenes passing outside the window of a moving train. Let them take you—without a word—where they will. To a memory. Or a feeling. Then tuck the book away. Save it for another day. And when you pick it up again, I pray that my journey sheds a little light on your own. And gentles you forward.

The time will come to cast off
    from the shore of all our fears

2

Bright Offerings

When my wife's Aunt Glenda died, a friend and I wrote a song called "A Ship Out of Water" to sing at her funeral. It begins:

This life is an island
Surrounded by eternity
You sailed away
Much too soon on that sea

Among the many she left behind were two young daughters and two sisters. Watching them grieve reminded me that the real pain of death is separation. A year and a half later,

I was reminded of this again when my Grandmother Myrtle left this world. Missing her so much is part of still loving her so deeply.

Those not yet initiated into the club of grieving may tell you—with good intention, no doubt—that separation from our loved ones is only temporary. When I was grieving, I tended to separate myself from the well-intentioned. They got on my nerves. Someone more mature in these things counseled me to be patient with those who were

not in the club. It's simply a region they have not yet traveled. And who would wish them there?

> *Memory is a country*
> *Where I can go to see your face*
> *But where can I go*
> *When I miss your embrace?*

Aunt Glenda and Grandmother Myrtle's departures also reminded me that the first part of grieving is tears. How did Jesus grieve? He wept. He let the pain of the death of his friend Lazarus overcome him. And he knew the separation was temporary. Even momentary.

> *Like a ship out of water*
> *You left me waiting here*
> *Longing just to be with you*
> *The time will come to cast off*
> *From the shore of all our fears*
> *And sail into the wild blue*
> *Wonder of Heaven*
> *And you'll be there*

So why put off the tears?

To be strong?

To exert a faith greater than Jesus had? No one is that strong. I have met people who as teenagers lost their dads and decades later fell down on the ground and finally wept over it.

Go on and cry a river. Let it rain down like tears from heaven. And let it cleanse and carry you to the arms of those who will be strong for you.

Most of the tears—especially early on—are, of course, tears for ourselves. It is pure love mixed liberally with self-pity over our loss and our needs that will no longer be met by the one we mourn.

When my fiancée died along with our future, I cried like the Mississippi in flood stage. A river for her family. A river for our dreams. And another river for my broken heart. I thought the rain would never end. Occasionally the cloud cover would break, only to darken again at the slightest lightning flash of memory. Then the tears flowed until the storm passed. I forgot what the stars and sky looked like. Little by little the storms became fewer and farther apart. The stars broke through. And many months later, after more than a year had passed, something happened. The tears began to change. And I hope and pray that this happens in you, too.

At some point—and it can be a long while in coming, in one of those moments when that certain song comes on the radio or when you round that familiar bend in the road where you walked, talked, ate, laughed, or played with the one who is now safe in the arms of heaven— as the agony of separation wells up inside you like a physical hurt—your tears will change. A certain alchemy like water into wine will occur. The tears will turn from reflections of misery to jewels of tribute. They will no longer be mostly streams of self-pity, but will shine with honor to the one you miss. All the self-pity may never be gone, just as the finest diamond has flaws that make it unique. But you will know when

it happens. You will have what C.S. Lewis called "clean and honest" agony, "good and tonic" moments. The sky will begin to clear. The color will creep back into the landscape.

And even before you are fully aware of it, a mysterious thing will happen. You will do what you fear most—let go a little more. A step back into the land of the living will logically seem like a step farther from the one you mourn. But in letting go—and this is the mysterious part—you will be moved nearer to, not farther from, the fields of heaven and the ones you know there. You will sense how thin the veil is between this world and the next—a curtain held up by only a string of heartbeats. And instead of wishing your heart to stop, the steadiness of your beating heart will call you back to this life like a universal Morse code.

That moment may not even be on the horizon yet. It is even farther away if you are fighting the tears. But when they begin to fall and the rainy season soaks you to the marrow,

every tear, along with the tender persuasion of those pulling for you on earth and in heaven, will bring that moment closer.

For me, that lifting point brought this awareness like a telegram from the other side and later found its way into Glenda's song.

If you could be here now
I think I know what you would say—
"Don't cry for me
I'm at Home and I'm safe"

Let all the tears that fall here
Turn to diamonds in God's hands—
Bright offerings
From life's Shadowlands

My friend walked right into
the agony with me.
That's what friends do.

3

Beside You in the Rain

I didn't know it at the time, but all those people who offered the acts of kindness I mentioned at the beginning of this letter were my tutors. They were my teachers in the school of sorrow. By being shipwrecked I learned why the Apostle James defined part of true religion as visiting those marooned among us. Somewhere along the line my visitors or rescuers had learned to offer comfort, perhaps because it had once been offered to them.

"Praise be to the God and Father of our Lord Jesus Christ, the Father of compassion and the God of all comfort, who comforts us in all our troubles, so that we can comfort those in any trouble with the comfort we ourselves have received from God." —2 Corinthians 1:3,4

Those who walked me through the first day of calamity, those who met me at the airport, came by my house, called, wrote, wept, and prayed—those who spent minutes or months with me—they comforted me. And I know they carried me. And you are being carried, too. As the road wound slowly on through the

valley of the shadow, so many events pointed me toward healing and to those who tended my wound or came alongside me to walk a mile and lighten the load. Some of them had been schooled by grief. Some had not. I am grateful to each of them.

In the winter after my fiancée died, a friend from college came to visit me. He had left his own family during the Christmas season in order to offer me comfort. My pain was still so fresh and I'm sure difficult to watch, but he came and stayed with me for three days.

On two afternoons we sat by the fire and he read to me from C.S. Lewis' journal *A Grief Observed*, written in the months after Lewis' wife died of cancer. It was hard but good to lean into lines like, "No one ever told me that grief felt so

On the ocean so lonesome
I was not left alone
Had some heavyweight friends
when my heart was a stone
And they carried the heartache
and made it their own
When the currents of sorrow
were strong

like fear," or, "There is an invisible blanket between me and the world." And, "Her absence is like the sky, spread over everything." It taught me that those in grief, no matter what kind of loss, have so much in common. My friend walked right into the agony with me. That's what friends do.

"A friend loves at all times, and a brother is born for adversity"
—Proverbs 17:17

Against the backdrop of a quick-fix world that wants you to get on with life (mainly because your grief makes them uncomfortable), one father told me, "This is a long valley. People will give you weeks or months to 'recover.' Give yourself a year at least. Maybe two. This is a wound God will help you manage. And you will occasionally bleed from it all your life, especially when you hear someone else's hard news. It will open that scar again—not to drag you back, but to move you to care for them." This man had lost a college-age son during a surgery to correct a heart disorder. Even though it had been nearly ten years since his son died, he told me that several times a year he walks out into the woods and loses it. He misses his son. That's what fathers do. And Someone carries them.

"There (in the desert) you saw how the LORD God carried you, as a father carries his son…"
—Deuteronomy 1:31

In early spring, another longtime buddy from college visited me. One night he forced me to wrestle him until, out of breath and begging for mercy, I cried uncle. We rolled on the floor laughing. The next day he sat me down and helped me make a list of goals. Long-range and short-range. From physical exercise to career goals like steps toward another recording project. Practical, spiritual, financial, and relationship goals. Everything from building a deck on my house to finding someone to compile tax information to reading the entire book of Psalms again. It took over two years to check off every item. I still have the list to remind me of the that time. And of that good friend.

> *"...there is a friend who sticks closer than a brother."—Proverbs 18:24*

I met a father and mother in Alaska a year after their twelve-year-old daughter went down in a small plane in the ocean. The father was the air traffic controller who took the Mayday call that his daughter's plane had run out of fuel. Another man, in his eighties, had schooled these parents in grief, telling them that we treat the dead badly in so many ways—like being reluctant to speak their names. We are overly cautious not to cause anyone in the land of the living undo distress, instead of allowing them the opportu-

nity to learn how to respond in a house of mourning. When we die, do we want everyone to tiptoe around our existence? This wise man, who had buried many loved ones, told the younger, grieving father, "When people ask you how many children you have, tell the whole truth. We have two—a son in high school and a daughter in heaven. And let the other person pursue or avoid reality." The future reality, in the biblical vision, is that one day those wounded parents will see their daughter again.

> *"And the sea gave up the dead that were in it..." —Revelation 20:13*

During my own shadowy time, the movies *Always* and *Ghost* pierced me to the core. I watched in agony as the spirits of the deceased lovers observed and tried to influence their grieving loved ones here on earth. Both stories are heartrending depictions of our deep longing and belief that love transcends death. If you haven't seen these movies, or have heard about and avoided them, it may be painful medicine at some point to rent one,

break out the tissues, and watch it with a good friend. (I recommend the original version of *Always,* starring Spencer Tracy.)

Aside from Solomon's words that the body returns to the dust and the spirit returns to God, I have no picture of how it really works on the other side. What kind of contact, if any, does God allow? (Certainly not nearly as much as Hollywood does.) Do the dead, or rather those living with God, still support us? We are told at least this much:

> *"…we are surrounded*
> *by such a great cloud of witnesses…"*
> *—Hebrews 12:1*

Will, my Grandmother Myrtle's first husband and childhood sweetheart, died in her arms on October 13, 1926. She was three months pregnant with my dad. She and Will had buried their three-year-old, Violet, in 1920. Myrtle remarried Alfred Raspberry Payne in 1931. She always told me that she respected Alfred but loved Will, and that in heaven she hoped Alfred understood, but she wanted to see Will first.

After my fiancée died, I spent a lot of hours with my Grandmother Myrtle on her porch swing. We sat. Holding hands. She told me stories. I asked her how she made it through after Will's death. She said some nights she prayed the sun would not come up the next day. But it always did. She told me things like, "Trouble comes to everyone, so best be happy while you can. Cry, then let it go. Why hurt yourself?" She was very practical and had a way of translating the Lord's truth into her own brand of Oklahoma faith.

On March 31, 1997, Myrtle joined Will, Violet, and Alfred. On April first, the sun came up. And I began loving my grandmother by missing her. That's what grandsons do. Her words and the thought of Grandmother in heaven with her mom and dad, eight brothers and sisters, Alfred, Violet, and Will helped me to take heart. It still does. That's what spiritual realities do.

"In this world you will have trouble. But take heart! I have overcome the world."
—Jesus, John 16:33

Well into the second year after RosaLynn's death, a good friend confronted me. He did it in a language I understood. Knowing my fondness for Robert Frost's poem about two roads diverging into a wood, he used that image to tell me I was in danger of choosing a road more traveled. He acknowledged that I had come through the darkest part of grief's valley. But he—and others—were concerned that I remained only partially alive. And that I was at a fork in the road. One road, the one less traveled, led back to life, to a renewed joy and vitality. The other led to a muted existence, where the outward signs of life masked a hardened, guarded, and potentially bitter heart.

Down the more traveled road I could be productive, even creative, but risked eventually turning into an eccentric old guy about whom the kids in the neighborhood all said,

"Don't go in Old Man Sprague's yard...he'll bite your head off. I hear something bad happened to him when he was young. And it warped him."

We laughed about that, but then my friend added with great tenderness, "All of us who love you are praying you will choose the other road. The one back to the Billy we know. It's a harder road, and maybe an act of God is involved, but you have to choose it, too. We're praying that you will." It is so difficult to refuse a scalpel so tenderly applied by a skillful friend. That day was a turning point. A fork in the road. I chose. And had to keep choosing. And it has made all the difference.

"Wounds from a friend can be trusted..."
—Proverbs 27:6

Have you ever had your own words turned back on you? I wrote a song years ago called "I Wish" for a high school graduation. It's one of those list songs. I wish you this. I wish you that. It's a prayer, really. A little more

than two years after my fiancée's death, I sang it as part of a concert at a singles conference. The speaker and everyone there knew my story. The following day I sat in to listen in on one of the speaker's sessions. Near the end of his very moving talk he announced that he was going to lead everyone in a song as a prayer for someone in the audience.

When the music began, it was "I Wish." Naturally, I was flattered. He took the microphone into the crowd. People began to sing along. He made his way to the back of the room where I sat in tears as over five hundred people sang my own words back to me. It was like all of heaven urging me onward.

In that moment the song changed voice—from my own to the brothers and sisters around me joined by the citizens of heaven, RosaLynn among them. And the life that had begun to grow again in my soul blossomed in a new way as they sang a prayer to me. I was

different. And I learned all over again—that's what prayers do.

I couldn't have known it then, but sitting in the row behind me was the woman who, two years later, would become my wife and the mother of our children.

I wish I could gather five hundred people around you to sing this prayer to you. In lieu of that, I offer it here, praying that you hear the heavenly chorus in your heart and among them the voice of the one you are missing most, singing you little by little back to life.

Jesus said, "Blessed are those who mourn for they shall be comforted." But how? By his words. By his Spirit moving in the darkest recesses of our own hearts and in the hearts and hands and arms of the comforters he sends. Hearts full of compassion. Hands full of food and willing to help. And arms open to hold your hurting heart. That's what hearts and hands and arms do best. They come alongside you in the storm when your

I wish you joy—I wish you peace
I wish you all the good
   that you have been to me
I hope you find what your heart is dreaming of
But most of all my friend for you
I wish you love

I wish you warm—when hearts are cold
I wish you light when there is darkness in your soul
I wish you strength for the facing of each day
But most of all I wish you love along the way

I wish you bold in your belief
I wish you well from all the scars the world can leave
And I wish you home in the Father's house one day
But most of all I wish you love
May you always have enough
Most of all I wish you love to find the way

own hands and arms cannot keep your heavy heart afloat. Let them carry you. And one day you may be called upon to return the comfort. And you will go there willingly, well-qualified, and able to say:

I never will forget
All of your kindness
When I was drowning in sorrow
Now that the flood is yours
No need to face it alone,
Oh, if I could make it all right,
You know I'd take the hurt away

I'd paint a yellow sun
Up in a big blue sky
Over the kind of world
That doesn't make you cry
And I'd be there with you
You would be smiling too
But till the sun comes out again
I'll walk beside you in the rain

I reason, that in Heaven—
Somehow, it will be even
Some new equation, given—
But, what of that?

4

Harvesting a Vacant Lot

During my stormiest grief, a distant friend became very close. In fact, she crossed a century to comfort me. I rediscovered the poetry of a shining soul well-acquainted with grief, Emily Dickinson.

Over a nine-year period she mourned her father, two dear friends, her mother, a nephew, and a man for whom she quietly held strong romantic feelings for many years. Her words mirrored my own thoughts and feelings.

I reason, Earth is short—
And Anguish —absolute—
And many hurt,
But, what of that?

I reason, we could die—
The best Vitality
Cannot excel Decay,
But what of that?

I reason, that in Heaven—
Somehow, it will be even—
Some new Equation, given—
But, what of that?

—Emily Dickinson (#301)

I'll tell you "what of that," Emily. It hurts. That's what. Life hurts.

And I think that's exactly what my favorite American poet was getting at. In the face of suffering, logic, reality, even the promises of Heaven, can all turn into Job's ineffectual friends, especially when accompanied by well-meaning, quick-fix evangelical platitudes. The numbing cocoon of loss or pain cannot be brushed aside by glib references to Romans 8:28, "All things work for good..." or, "This too shall pass" or the sardonic homespun quip, "Oh, well, in a hundred years we'll all be dead anyway."

True as those are, when pain prowls inside you like a panther, the shortest verse in the New Testament becomes the mightiest: "Jesus wept." Jesus knew life was brief. He knew anguish and death and loss were inescapable realities in this world. He knew he himself would "excel decay," beat death, and thereby bring a "new equation" into the cosmos by factoring in resurrection and eternal life for all who would believe. He knew all this. And yet Jesus stood at the graveside of his dear friend Lazarus, knowing he would raise him from the grave in ten minutes, and wept. He wept bitterly. It hurt.

In November of 1989 I stood at the graveside of RosaLynn. We would have been married the next spring. But in a split second, in the time it takes to peek around a van to see if the road is clear to pass, she was gone. Divine ricochet? Or guardian angel on a smoke break?

I know life is short. I know death comes to us all. I carry the unshakable belief and hope that in heaven "it will all be even." But on this side there is real loss, and for so many who must trudge through a winter of loss— not only from death, but loss of any kind— there is a cruel, mathematic-like net deficit in the equation of life. "The masses of men lead lives of quiet desperation," Thoreau said. And to avoid deficit living, he moved off into the woods.

I moved to a vacant lot, at least emotionally. All the dreams and plans and longings were leveled to the horizon and beyond. The season in my heart changed to winter and refused to allow spring to come for over two years. Out of the sheer pain and shock, the whys and what ifs, the sleepless nights, the wrestling match with God, the test of faith, two questions emerged. The first, simply one of survival: Is there a way through? The second, which came much later: Is there a way back? To life? To feeling? To joy? Or would I become one among the masses, quietly desperate, subtly (or openly) cynical, trudging toward the ultimate and only relief, death and heaven beyond?

It is only by the grace of God and many heavyweight friends that I can now answer yes to both questions. There was no quick fix. There is no short answer. I can only give you some glimpses of that long and winding road.

I found myself in the same wrestling match

that C.S. Lewis described in *A Grief Observed*. He wrote, "Not that I am in much danger of ceasing to believe in God. The real danger is of coming to believe such dreadful things about Him...What reason have we, except our own desperate wishes, to believe that God is, by any standard we can conceive, 'good'?"

Since early 1988 I have been singing a song I wrote called "La Vie (Life)." In it are two lines in French, which I was told the Christians in France use quite often. "La vie est dure, mais Dieu est bon." Life is hard, but God is good. Like Lewis, I wondered, "Doesn't all the...evidence suggest exactly the opposite?" Doesn't RosaLynn's death and all the net deficit in the hurting world prove a net deficit in the God I had leaned on for so many years?

Looking back, I can see the test of faith more clearly. It was a not-so-simple fill-in-the-blank. Life is hard, but God is _____ ?

Several weeks after the accident, sometime around at Christmas, one of my brothers came to my bedside and said, "Why don't you go do what you want now? You've done it God's way, and look what you get."

He was angry for me. I lay there lifeless, my head shaven from grief, a truly sad sight. I remember listlessly saying to him, "Where else am I gonna go? Should I sell books in the airports with the Krishnas? I wouldn't look good in saffron sheets." His remark filled in the blank with a logical, cynical answer based on the apparent evidence, and many people conclude just this: Life is hard, but God is <u>unreliable</u>.

Just after Christmas of that year I was standing by Rose's grave with her father, one of her brothers, and one of her sisters. The winter wind was slicing through us, but we hardly noticed. A car stopped a short way from us and a man got out. He was over fifty, short, his hair and bushy mustache graying. He looked a little like Old Man Winter him-

self. When he saw who we were, he headed directly for Rose's father, his old brown coat flying open, both arms extended wide and tears streaming down his face. As he approached, his eyes never left Dr. Olivares. He spoke in anguish, raising his voice so it would carry above the wind loud in the branches above us. And he said this: "I'm so sorry you have to hurt this way." Those were the first words that pierced my numb heart, and I will never forget them. Only later I found out that the man was also a doctor, a colleague of Rose's father, and had lost his wife the previous year.

Through all the impenetrable silence from heaven, the hollow days, the listless hours, the deep, unanswered agonies, the "mad midnight moments," as Lewis called them, I carried the image of that man and his words in my heart, I suppose because I must know that God, though silent, hurts, too. Jesus wept. That doesn't unravel the whys and what ifs, but it changes everything. Life is hard, but God is <u>tenderhearted</u>. (Or at least,

not indifferent or unmoved.)

In February of 1990 I sang and spoke at my first event since Rose died. A single's conference—the last place I wanted to be, especially grieving over a dead fiancée. After one of my sessions a brave and tender soul came up to speak with me. She offered me the first Scripture that actually stuck to my soul. It was from Ecclesiastes, not the perkiest book of the Bible: "It is better to go to a house of mourning than to go to a house of feasting, for death is the destiny of every man, and the living should take this to heart" (Ecclesiastes 7:2). She explained that it is not more fun in the house of mourning, but it is better because the perspective is as crystal-clear as it gets in this world. There is a certain creeping cluelessness about prosperity that deep loss will not allow. This woman said that my perspective would be keener and more farsighted than it had ever been. If perspective came with such a high price tag, I wasn't sure I wanted it. But she had the credibility of a calm soul, well-acquainted with

suffering yet not sad. I took in her words like a starving pilgrim. Life is hard, but God is <u>wise</u>.

During that time Emily's poems continued to echo my own experience. I ran into lines like, "There is a pain so utter it swallows substance up" (#599), and "You left me, Sire, two Legacies/ A Legacy of Love/...You left me Boundaries of Pain/ Capacious as the Sea/ Between Eternity and Time/ Your Consciousness—and Me" (#644), and "How happy I was if I could forget/ To remember how sad I am" (#898). I read her poetry daily and for three weeks dug worms morning and night for a little robin that had fallen out of a nest into my backyard until, shortly after I released *Pocotera* (Littlewing), I found this one:

> *If I can stop one heart from breaking*
> *I shall not live in vain*
> *If I can ease one Life the Aching*
> *Or cool one Pain*
> *Or help one fainting Robin*

Unto his Nest again
I shall not live in Vain. (#919)

Just when I was wondering if God had vacated the universe for happier climes, I actually laughed. Real laughter. And real, cleansing tears.

Emily said more: "I shall know why—when Time is over/ And I have ceased to wonder why/ Christ will explain each separate anguish/ In the fair schoolroom of the sky" (#193), and "This World is not Conclusion/ A Species stands beyond/ Invisible, as Music/ But positive, as Sound..." (#501). But what of that? A little bird? A long dead poet of passion and faith? Evidence? Of what? How would Emily fill in the blank? Life is hard, but God is "visible in all circumstances" (#820) or simply "our Old Neighbor" (#623).

That summer a friend's grandmother wrote me. During World War II Marion Brady had faced what so many had. The khaki-colored car pulled up in front of her house. The somber officer came to the door and handed her the dreaded telegram which began, "We regret to inform you..." Her husband had been killed at sea. She never remarried; she raised her children and endured. Some of her words to me were these: "The pain will be less on the cutting edge in time. You have been given great gifts by God. You can use them in dedication and devotion to your young lady, and the more you use them, the better you will feel."

I never met Mrs. Brady, though we spoke on the telephone and wrote a couple of times. She had a delightful, even outrageous, sense of humor. She helped show me there was a way through. The more I sang and wrote and wrestled, the better I felt. Mrs. Brady died and joined Mr. Brady in December of 1993. She filled in the blank something like this: Life is hard, but God is faithful and practical.

Dozens of small incidents, flashes of understanding—"twigs of evidence," as Emily called them—occurred along the way.

One Sunday afternoon on a rebroadcast of a William F. Buckley interview with Malcolm Muggeridge, the topic was faith. Mr. Muggeridge quoted King Lear as one of the most concise definitions of faith he had ever heard. In the final act when Lear's daughter Cordelia is wondering why all the suffering was inflicted on her dying father, the blinded King tells her we must "take upon ourselves the mystery of things" (V. iii.16). Life is hard, but God is <u>deliberately silent for his own inscrutable reasons</u>.

About the same time, something I had read many times struck me with greater force than ever—Paul's letter to the Thessalonians.

"…we do not want you to be ignorant about those who fall asleep, or to grieve like the rest of men, who have no hope. We believe that Jesus died and rose again and so we believe that God will bring with Jesus those who have fallen asleep in him. According to the Lord's own word, we who are still alive, who are left till the coming of the Lord, will certainly not precede those who have fallen asleep. For the Lord himself will come down from heaven, with a loud command, with the voice of the archangel and with the trumpet call of God, and the dead in Christ will rise first. After that, we who are still alive and are left will be caught up together with them in the clouds to meet the Lord in the air. And so we will be with the Lord forever."
—*1 Thessalonians 4:13-18*

Life is hard, but God is <u>sovereign</u> (not nervous, has a specific long-range plan that is not irreparably derailed by the exit, untimely or otherwise, of any one from the planet).

I began to find twigs of evidence in such unexpected places. While reading the letters of Vincent van Gogh I found this statement of faith: "Sometimes the pilot of a ship can use a storm to make headway, instead of being wrecked by it." And I spent an entire night until dawn painting it in large gold letters on my bedroom wall so I could read it

every morning. Life is hard, but God is <u>able and resourceful</u>.

About a year and a half had passed when, after a concert in Florida, I met a woman who came to hear my music because she had heard my story. She was curious to know how I was making it. Her fiancé had died of a heart attack fifteen years earlier. She had found a way through, but not a way back. We talked for several hours. In college she had studied philosophy and decided existentialism was the bravest system of thought and belief with which to face reality—the "what you see is all you get" approach. We compared notes on the landscape of our tragedies. After fifteen years she was still hard as nails and mad at the cosmos. So I asked her, "How is that philosophy working for you?"

She said something I will never forget: "I have found that applying philosophy to the reality of death is like swallowing an elephant. It just won't go down." She had spent fifteen long, painful years in self-protection and wounded isolation. She had not loved again nor married. She had filled in the blank: Life is hard, but God is <u>absent</u>.

As time trudged on I discovered there really was a way through. I wrote songs, traveled, made homemade ice cream, took mission trips, scuba dived, grew tomatoes, and recorded an album, "Torn Between Two Worlds." The question remained: Is there a way back? My friends were still wondering. And so was I. Was it possible for all the "twigs of evidence" scattered along the way to take root, sprout, and blossom again in such a vacant lot? Life is hard, but is God that good a gardener?

I was in Amsterdam one evening, on the way home from a mission trip to Sweden, when I talked with a young woman, Yvette, who I hadn't seen in nearly six years. Her zeal for God and characteristic Dutch frankness helped me turn a silent corner, though she probably doesn't know it. During our conversation she looked up at me from the floor where she sat and blurted out, "So, Billy, will you ever marry?" (The questions behind the question were, "Are you moving on? Are you coming back to life?") I squirmed a bit and dodged the question, saying basically I don't know and my heart is not at that place yet and I don't know the future, etc.

Then with great tenderness she looked up at me and said, "Well, Billy, I know there is at least one person in heaven who wants you to be very happy." I couldn't fight that kind of eternal perspective. I knew immediately Yvette was right. RosaLynn was not the kind of person who would appreciate a shrine of melancholy built to her memory, a shrine in which I would protect myself from life. The temptation to build one was very real. But in fact, she would be very irritated by that scenario. Those we mourn are more honored by our pressing on. The undodgeable power of that reality worked on my stiff heart like strong hands. The blood flowed into aban-

doned places inside me like rain on dry ground. Life is hard, but <u>God, and the citizens of heaven, are for us</u>.

In July of 1992 I went to Barcelona on a mission trip and another conversation reshaped my insides. I am still so grateful to my Dutch friend, Tjiebbo (pronounced "Chebo," who is as discerning as Yvette—and more frank). One of the guest speakers asked the question, "What do we do with our personal pain, which we all have, in regard to our mission in life?" Do we get well and then get on with our calling? Or do we respond to our calling and get well along the way? His counsel was b) get well along the way. We are all wounded. If we wait until we are well to be fit for our mission, life will be over. He concluded by asking us to turn to those near us and ask for prayer for a very specific pain in our life. I turned to my Dutch friend who knew me from two previous trips together in Sweden. I told him I was coming back to life, functional and even thriving, able to enjoy so much and be useful and productive. But I described to him the twisted knot inside me about Rose's abrupt, and what I sometimes called rude, departure from the planet. It was a hard-to-reach mess of tangled, long-term sorrow and disappointment with life and the way God runs (or allows) the universe to run.

No doubt, the knot was stubborn strands of anger, bitterness, mistrust, confusion, and a sense of betrayal or unrightness about her death. And I didn't know how to untie them. My friend prayed two sentences: "Dear Lord, don't let Billy's memories remain anchors that he has to drag along. Turn them to treasures he can carry with him." I began to feel the warm tears gather in my eyes and then drip onto my hands. I wept gently. No tumult. No great upheaval.

That's all Tjiebbo prayed. We sat in silence for a minute or so. He then counseled me to recheck and let go of any unspoken "vows" I may have made, like "remaining single" or "finding a manageable level of melancholy" (Thoreau's "quiet desperation") instead of

coming fully back to the land of the living.

In less than fifteen minutes I was different. Lighter. The knot in my soul was gone. I took a deeper breath than I had taken in over two years. The most surprising thing of all is what replaced the knot. Gratitude. I was actually grateful. For RosaLynn. For knowing her. For loving and being loved. For the time we had. And I was thankful for the tenacious love of so many along the way. And thankful to God, who in those moments answered so many prayers. After my friend's short prayer asking God to turn my memories into treasures, not anchors, and the deep comfort and release that happened, how could I resign myself to deficit living? How could I settle for a manageable level of melancholy? I still remember taking in a breath of life all the way down to my toenails. The last of the heavy load dropped away. And the long, narrow valley of grief widened into the open plains of possibility. Life is hard, but God is <u>a redeemer</u> (and he knows tangled knots better than all the Boy Scouts and sailors in the world).

Since then I have written hundreds of songs, traveled a million miles, made a mountain of homemade ice cream, taken mission trips, scuba dived, grown tomatoes, completed two more recordings, started oil painting, written books, and fallen in love with and married a precious, life-savoring woman named Kellie, surely one of the bravest people on the planet. At this writing we have two twigs of merciful evidence of heaven's influence and reality, Willow and Wyatt.

God did what I thought beyond the reaches of even his death-defying power. He harvested my vacant lot. In the test of faith, he filled in the blank with his own goodness. And I am convinced that the way we fill in that blank, "Life is hard, but God is _____," largely determines the quality of our lives, the peace of our minds, the health of our hearts, the calm of our souls, and the pace of our steps.

Emily was right. Earth is short. Anguish is

absolute. Vincent was right. A good ship's pilot can use a storm to make headway. Paul was right, too. We grieve over real loss with real tears but with real hope. And Marion was right. And so were Yvette and Tjiebbo and Shakespeare. And my favorite Hebrew poet said it better than I have:

"He reached down from on high and took hold of me; he drew me out of deep waters. He rescued me from my powerful enemy, From my foes, who were too strong for me. They confronted me in the day of my disaster, but the LORD was my support. He brought me out into a spacious place…"
—Psalm 18:16-19

King David would agree with the French believer: Life is hard, but God is <u>good</u>, <u>very good</u>.

He walked that
lonesome valley...
and made a way through it
for all of us...

5

A Spacious Place

I am sorry this narrow valley is part of your story. This uninvited shadowland will always be part of the landscape of my life. And yours. It is a prison cell and a haven. A blind alley and a pathway. In it you can find stormy and still water. Bitter and painfully sweet memories. A vacant lot and green pastures. Agony and rest.

And in it you can find the great Comforter, the man of sorrows, who is well-acquainted with grief—abandonment—and separation. He walked that lonesome valley, as the old song goes, and made a way through it for all of us. Not just to the foothills of heaven, beyond death, but to a spacious place again, here on this side of heaven. To an expanding horizon in the chapters following this one in your life. A place you may not believe possible right now, where light grows, irresistible, like the dawn, and your dormant heart stirs. Your pulse quickens. And, at long last, winter yields.

This chapter of your life will, of course, color the rest of your story—with the winnowed colors of a renewed passion in your soul, with a fire-tested awareness of the immeasurable value of one irreplaceable person. Your heart will remain crowded with those you love and who love you. Those walking beside you. And those waiting ahead, around the final bend, in the foothills of heaven.

Why does God permit such a deep wound and the dark night of the soul that so often follows? Would we look to the light without the dark? Did we bring death on ourselves as the Eden story says? I don't know. I don't presume to know. But I have a firsthand account that he rescued me from the valley of the shadow of death. And I have more than a subtle clue why he did. The very next verse in Psalm 18 tells plainly why God rescues us from grief and calamity. It's not theological. It's not philosophical. It's because of who we are to him. And how he regards us.

> "...he rescued me because
> He delighted in me."
> —Psalm 18:19

That one word can melt a heart. It did mine. And it moved me miles down the road to see that God isn't angry with me or you, or untouched or cavalier about our suffering, or tired of our tears, impatient with our lack of understanding or thrown off if, in our pain, we turn cold hearts to him. He loves us. He loves you. I've heard that thousands of times. But He *delights* in me? And in you? That is an energy of love I can only compare to how I feel about my own children. I delight in them.

That's how much I love them. And that's what our Heavenly Father does. He delights in us. And he moves "close to the brokenhearted and saves those who are crushed in spirit" (Psalm 34:18). He moves close because God knows what it's like to lose someone. He lost a son. But not for forever.

God loves you. It comes down to that. Maybe that's what I should have told you first. But even the sound of that great reality can ring hollow in the grand canyon of sorrow. For me, that tender, divine love was at first more real in all the acts of kindness extended to me than in just those three words alone. In fact, looking back, I can see that all the kindnesses from friends and strangers, the wise words and prayers, even a baby bird falling into my yard, were expressions of the love of God reaching me, carrying me, and comforting me. I think that's what you will find, too. God's love will show itself around you in small ways. And little by little, that great love will grow like the dawn, warm you, and draw you forward toward the horizon.

God, the Father of us all, and no stranger to a wounded heart, loves you. And someday this canyon that he is bringing you through will be a monument to the power of that love.

Take heart, wounded friend. Take time to grieve, but grieve with hope. Cry a river. An ocean if you like. Take a hand kindly offered. Help one fainting robin. Keep tying your shoes. Read the Psalms or have someone read them to you. Find some good walking companions. And some good traveling songs. Here is one of mine. Sometimes I hear it sung from earth to heaven. Sometimes I think it's what those already there are singing to us.

I don't want to let you go
I don't want to say goodbye
But the road has led us here to this divide
Nothing I can say or do
Can make it any other way
But the promise of forever knows no time
*   or space*
And out there in the somewhere I will pray
And speak your name…Every day to heaven

Now Go, shine like a star
Knowing our hearts can never really be apart
Fly as high as you can
And it won't be long
'Til I see you again

What is meant to be is such a mystery.
And mysteries are not meant to understand
The hardest part of love has got to be
Leaving it in bigger hands

Enough words. Forgive me if I've said too much. And so, "until the day dawns and the morning star rises in your heart" (2 Peter 1:19), I leave you in bigger hands.

Fly as high as you can
and it won't be long
'Til I see you again